Slavery, Antislavery, and the Underground Railroad:
A Dutchess County Guide

Slavery, Antislavery, and the Underground Railroad:
A Dutchess County Guide

Researched and written by
members of the Mid-Hudson Antislavery History Project
under the direction of Dr. F. Kennon Moody

Copyright © 2010 by Mid-Hudson Antislavery History Project
All rights reserved. No part of this publication may be reproduced, stored in or introduced into a retrieval system, or transmitted in any form, or by any means (electronic, mechanical, photocopying, recording, or otherwise), without the prior written permission of both the copyright owner and the publisher of this book. For information, address Hudson House Publishing.

ISBN 978-1-58776-908-5
Library of Congress Control Number: 2010921895

Manufactured in the United States of America
Netpublications, Inc.
675 Dutchess Turnpike, Poughkeepsie, NY 12603
www.hudsonhousepub.com (800) 724-1100

Design by Holly Wahlberg
Cover image © Betsy Braun Lane 2008
Maps by Tony Moore of Moore Creative Designs

Table of Contents

SLAVERY AND ANTISLAVERY IN DUTCHESS COUNTY: AN INTRODUCTION 1

SITE MAPS 22-23

THE QUAKER TRAIL (EASTERN DUTCHESS) 24

1 Storm Family Slave Cemetery, East Fishkill 24
2 The Community of Freemanville, Union Vale 26
3 Oblong Meeting House, Quaker Hill, Pawling 28
4 Nine Partners Meeting House, Millbrook 32
5 Oswego Meeting House, Moores Mill 35

THE RIVER TRAIL (WESTERN DUTCHESS) 36

6 Mt. Gulian Historic Site, Beacon 36
7 The Community of Baxtertown 38
8 First Congregational Church, Poughkeepsie 40
9 Smith Metropolitan AME Zion Church, Poughkeepsie 42
10 Colored Lancaster School, Poughkeepsie 44
11 Second Baptist Church (formerly First Congregational), Poughkeepsie 46
12 Former Site of John Bolding Home, Poughkeepsie 46
13 St. James Episcopal Church, Hyde Park 48
14 Quitman House, Rhinebeck 50
15 Rhinebeck Cemetery 51

Notes 53
Sources and Suggested Reading 56

Preface

The Mid-Hudson Antislavery History Project

The people of Dutchess and Ulster counties played unique and significant roles in the history of American slavery and abolitionism. The Hudson Valley made more concentrated use of enslaved agricultural labor than almost any area in the North. But Dutchess and Ulster also played significant roles in the Underground Railroad and the public abolitionist movement. The Mid-Hudson Antislavery History Project (MHAHP) works to call attention to this neglected aspect of our past. Created in 2006, MHAHP brings together scholars, independent researchers, educators, civic leaders, and interested community members. Our goals are:

• to conduct and synthesize research on the history of antislavery in the Mid-Hudson Valley, with special emphasis on the Underground Railroad

• to interpret this history and share these interpretations with an array of residents and visitors in our area, and in particular with students and youth

• to place local history in the broad contexts of racial slavery in the New World, the African American experience, and the legacies of antislavery today, including the impact of this historic grassroots movement on subsequent struggles for racial and social justice

This guidebook introduces Dutchess residents and visitors to key sites in the county that were associated with slavery, the abolitionist movement, and the Underground Railroad. It is not a comprehensive guide. We have focused on sites that are both significant and publicly accessible, and whose histories are already well researched. We hope to publish expanded editions, in the future, as our research continues.

We invite you to join us in that work. MHAHP is a volunteer, grassroots organization that welcomes members and supporters of all backgrounds. We are a donor-advised fund of the Community Foundation of Dutchess County, supported by individual contributions. Proceeds from this guide will further our research, public interpretation, and living history re-enactment.

The Mid-Hudson Antislavery History Project would like to offer heartfelt thanks to Christopher Densmore, archivist at Swarthmore College, for his gracious assistance in researching Quaker records; Professor Edythe Quinn of Hartwick College, for sharing her research on African American life in the Hudson Valley; Kathy Moyer for sharing her research on the Nine Partners Friends Meeting and School; and Daniel Jones and Fred Roe for assistance with maps and images.

Slavery and Antislavery in the Hudson Valley: An Introduction

Two Centuries of Slavery

As part of New York's agricultural heartland, the Hudson Valley was one of the most significant sites of slavery north of the Mason-Dixon line. Slavery endured in New York from the 1620s until the 1820s. The state had a larger concentration of enslaved people than any other state north of Maryland, numbering 21,329 at the system's peak in 1790. The Hudson Valley was the major slaveholding region in New York, with 1,856 slaves in 1790 in Dutchess County alone. (At that time, the county's total population numbered a bit above 30,000.) [1]

The legacies of slavery in this area were considerable. Many of the Hudson Valley's stone houses, cleared fields, and open vistas bear silent witness to the labor of enslaved hands. The Valley contains many sites associated with slavery, including extant slave quarters behind some early homes. Most poignant, perhaps, are gravesites, including the Storm Family Slave Cemetery (site #1) and African American burials at Rhinebeck Cemetery (#15). One Rhinebeck stone marks the grave of "Jack – Native of Africa," who died in 1826. Such sites remind us that diverse West and South African peoples settled the Hudson Valley, through the operations of the international slave trade. The Valley's heritage is thus not only Dutch and English, but also African, from the earliest days.

With its history of slavery, the Hudson Valley was notorious for its hostility toward abolitionists, even at the height of antislavery activism in the nineteenth century. "Most places on the Hudson River," declared abolitionist Samuel Ringgold Ward, were "thoroughly and hopelessly pro-slavery." The Quitman House (site #14) is a particularly vivid example of ties between North and South. John Quitman, born in this house, moved to Mississippi where he became an extremely wealthy cotton planter, the owner of hundreds of slaves, and a prominent secessionist politician.

Early Hudson Valley newspapers often carried advertisements for the return of enslaved people who had escaped. This one, in which an Ulster slaveholder offered ten dollars and expenses for the return of a man named "James," appeared in the *Poughkeepsie County Journal*, 9 December 1788.

Ten Dollars Reward.

RUN-AWAY from the subscriber about the 8th Nov. instant, a NEGRO MAN named JAMES, about five feet ten inches high, 27 or 28 years of age, a rugged, well built fellow; had on when he went away, a brown coloured coat and waistcoat of home made filled cloth, and blue breeches; he speaks English and Dutch, and stammers a little when he speaks.—— Whoever apprehends the said Negro, and secures him in any gaol, so that the subscriber, (living at Rochester, Ulster county, and State of New.York) may get him again, shall be entitled to the above reward, and reasonable charges.
DERICK WESBROOK

This case, from the minutes of the New York Manumission Society records at the New-York Historical Society, offers evidence that American Indians as well as African Americans were enslaved in Dutchess. Willet Seaman was a Quaker member of the Manumission Society. The outcome of the Society's action is not known.

Willet Seaman represented the case of Jenny, an Indian Woman, whose son is claimed as a slave of John Brenson, Jr. of Dutchess County. Resolved after hearing the circumstances relating to the above case that the above-mentioned Boy is free and that the Society defend him against any attempts that may be made to deprive him of said Liberty, and that Willet Seaman be requested to inform the said John Brenson of this Resolution and to support the Mother in bringing forward a suit to recover the wages due to the said Boy, provided a suit is commenced by said Brenson.

Gradual Emancipation in New York

In 1785, amid the heady aftermath of the American Revolution, New York banned the further importation of slaves for sale. After 1788, the state permitted slave owners to manumit their human property (that is, make an individual decision to release slaves from bondage). Though the Revolution did not end slavery in the new United States, it prompted many Northern states to move toward ending slavery.

Despite resistance from slaveholders, a 1799 New York law finally provided for a process of gradual abolition. All enslaved children born after July 4, 1799, were to be freed at the age of twenty-eight for men and twenty-five for women. The state legislature removed the final legal barriers to freedom in 1817, decreeing that all slaves born before July 4, 1799, would receive their freedom on July 4, 1827.

During these decades the rate of manumission in Dutchess County increased, but despite this, the role of slavery changed slowly.[2] Slave owners who included manumission in their wills often added qualifications: manumission was not always immediate upon the death of the owner, but sometimes depended on a slave serving further years, as property of those who inherited the estate. Sometimes manumission came only after the enslaved man or woman had essentially purchased his or her freedom through additional labor.

Prior to 1827, not all African Americans in the Hudson Valley were enslaved. In Dutchess County, the presence of many free Blacks created vibrant communities that served as early sites of resistance and protest. Among the most important free African American communities were Freemanville (site #2), Baxtertown (#7), and the Guinea Community (associated with St. James Church, #13). MHAHP is conducting research on the life stories of several individuals and families who escaped slavery and settled in Dutchess, including James Freeman of Freemanville and James F. Brown, who escaped from enslavement in Maryland and worked for the Verplanck family at Mt. Gulian in Beacon (site # 6).

Throughout the antebellum period, the Mid-Hudson Valley was not a safe place for fugitive slaves and freedom-seekers. Even as the state moved toward abolition and some masters chose manumission, interest in apprehending fugitive slaves increased. In the Town of Shawangunk, on the west side of the Hudson, local slaveholders organized the Society for the Apprehending of Slaves in 1796. The Society evidently maintained a list of slaves belonging to the families who became members of the society. When any such family felt a slave was acting in a way that suggested he meant to run away, they notified the president of the society. Eight members were designated "riders" to apprehend and return the runaways if possible.[3] Thus, the Underground Railroad originally sprang up in Dutchess and Ulster Counties to aid local freedom-seekers in their quest for refuge.

This gravestone at the Rhinebeck Cemetery, marks the resting place of Bailey Johnson, who died free in 1834 but had been born in slavery.

This portrait of Richard Jenkins was discovered at the St. James Episcopal Church by researchers studying the church's cemetery in Hyde Park, where Jenkins is buried. Jenkins obtained his freedom and worked as church-sexton for many years.

Quakers and Slavery

Eastern Dutchess, containing America's largest Quaker settlement outside Philadelphia, played a leading role in ending slavery among members of the Society of Friends. From an early date, Quakers in Dutchess County operated an Underground Railroad to help freedom-seekers reach safe havens further north. In the decade after 1785, slaves in Dutchess County absconded at an average rate of five per year.[4]

In this guidebook the Quaker Trail, which runs through the eastern part of Dutchess County, includes three meeting houses of the Society of Friends: Oblong Meeting House (site #3), Nine Partners Meeting House (#4), and Oswego Meeting House (#5). All three had important associations with the antislavery cause. These were by no means the only Friends meetings in Dutchess County. The Mid-Hudson Antislavery History Project is also researching antislavery members and activities in the Creek Meeting, Crum Elbow Meeting, Poughkeepsie Meeting, and others in the county, as well as possible Underground Railroad connections to Milton Friends Meeting in Ulster and Friends in Westchester, Putnam, Columbia, and beyond.

Though New York Quakers were early opponents of slavery, their actual relationship with the institution and with African Americans was complicated, since many owned slaves themselves. In the 1750s, well before the American Revolution, a reformist spirit appeared among New York Friends, who took an early lead among Quakers in debating abolition. As historians have recently noted:

> Unlike Friends in some other colonies, New York
> Quakers did not own large numbers of slaves. Farmers
> on Long Island and in the Hudson River Valley held
> slaves, but not in the numbers to be found in Newport,
> Philadelphia, or the West Indies. Thus the moral dilemma
> of having slaves and the financial impact of freeing them
> was less in New York than in many other centers.[5]

At the New York Yearly Meetings of the Society of Friends slavery was a prevalent topic. On a local level, communities of Friends also held monthly meetings, where Friends "would apply for permission to marry, to move away from the meeting, for relief if they were in difficult circumstances, and for any projects or concerns that they had."[6] At these meetings, Friends who opposed slavery urged all Quakers to reject the institution.

But some Friends had developed a great dependence on their slaves, leading them to resist this antislavery sentiment. Always, in Quaker debates, there remained the question of the future role and well-being of slaves who were released. Historian Michael Groth, in his study of Dutchess County, notes the lack of unanimity among Quakers:

> Friends in Dutchess County were not unanimous in their condemnation of slavery; while condemning the trafficking of slaves, members were slow to emancipate those already held in bondage. Furthermore, Quakers constituted a distinct minority in Dutchess, and their pacifism during the Revolution alienated them even further from the rest of society.[7]

As the nineteenth century began, New York Quakers actively advocated for the manumission of slaves and many joined the New York Manumission Society. As we will see in the guide to individual sites, many Quakers went further, publicly denouncing slavery and helping individual freedom-seekers on their journeys north.

This image of Quakers at worship at Oblong Friends Meeting, captures something of the spirit of old-style Quakerism in the county. From Warren H. Wilson, *Quaker Hill: A Sociological Study* (1907).

The Underground Railroad

Those who aided fugitives operated secretly in the Hudson Valley, even after slavery ended in New York. Dutchess County's proximity to New York City (which had strong commercial ties to the South) made publicity risky, even as late as the Civil War era. But it appears that many fugitives traveled to New York City, where the Vigilance Committee of David Ruggles was the center of the Underground Railroad's operations. Ruggles and other allies sent fugitives up through the Hudson Valley, sometimes by barge or steamboat to Albany or Troy. Other fugitives traveled through the eastern side of Dutchess, passing through the chain of Quaker communities that extended from New York City into Massachusetts or Vermont. Those who reached Vermont might have contact with Quaker abolitionist Rowland T. Robinson, who earlier had attended the Nine Partners School in Dutchess. Some freedom-seekers went to Central or Western New York – most likely via the Erie Canal – to Oswego or farther west to Rochester or Buffalo. After passage of a stringent Fugitive Slave Law in 1850, many continued on to Canada.

Historians currently estimate that, nationwide, the Underground Railroad helped approximately 100,000 fugitives reach freedom. The impact of this grassroots movement should not be underestimated. Among other things, it was an early, radical example of interracial cooperation in the cause of justice, and one that was largely erased from national memory after the Civil War, during the era of sectional reconciliation. Many grassroots abolitionists – especially women, who lacked political and voting rights – became enthusiastic supporters of the Railroad. To some, abolishing slavery seemed like a distant or impossible goal; helping specific individuals reach freedom was a modest but tangible victory.[8]

It is important, however, to place the Underground Railroad in context. Its "conductors," despite effort and risk, freed only a tiny fraction of enslaved people. The majority of white Northerners did not support the road, and it seldom ran "underground" in any literal sense. The Mid-Hudson Antislavery History Project is investigating several houses in Dutchess that may have harbored freedom-seekers. The most important evidence of this is not secret rooms or tunnels, but documented links to free Blacks, Quakers, or abolitionists who were owners or tenants. Most tunnels or secret hideaways in local historic properties probably had other uses: smuggling goods along the Hudson, protecting "wanted" men (both Patriots and Loyalists) during the American Revolution, or even hiding valuable foods and wines. In some colonial houses, small basement rooms served as living quarters for servants and slaves.

A few fragmentary written records show that the Underground Railroad ran through Poughkeepsie, at least in later years. In his narrative of his escape from slavery in North Carolina, Moses Roper reported that he received medical care from a woman in Poughkeepsie, during his flight north. According to a remarkable account in the Poughkeepsie Eagle in December 1860, another fugitive had been born a free man in Ulster County, but while working as a sailor he had been "seized and confined, and eventually sold to a New Orleans trader." After ten years of enslavement in Louisiana, the man stowed away on a ship and made it back to New York. Two others escaped with him on the ship from New Orleans; the Eagle reported that they were "already on their way to Canada via the Underground Railroad." [9]

George W. Sterling, owner of an iron factory at 23 Hamilton Street, is the only Poughkeepsie resident who was identified in a local obituary as having been active in "managing the machinery of the underground railroad by which escaping slaves, after the passage of the Fugitive Slave Law, were sent through to Canada." [10] George and his wife Emeline Sterling had their home at 121 Cannon Street (no longer extant). After the Civil War, Emeline was the benefactress of the Sterling School in Greenville, South Carolina. She gave money to Daniel M. Minus, a teacher who was born in slavery, to help found the school for freedmen and women.[11]

Quakers at the Nine Partners Meeting, in what is today Millbrook, probably played a role in assisting fugitives from slavery on their way to freedom.

Jacob and Deborah Willetts, members of the Nine Partners Friends Meeting in Millbrook, were almost certainly involved in Underground Railroad activities. Teachers at the Nine Partners School, they were both outspoken leaders among the county's Quaker abolitionists.

Public Antislavery Activism in Dutchess

In 1833, creation of the American Anti-Slavery Society in Boston marked the rise of a new, radical antislavery presence in the United States. Unlike earlier groups, members of the AASS called for immediate emancipation. They rejected compensation for slave masters and called for recognition of freed people, not as "Africans," but as citizens of the United States. Radical antislavery was extremely controversial and its advocates faced intense criticism and even violence across the North.

In the Hudson Valley, Dutchess County was an outpost of radical antislavery. Sites on the River Trail, which runs through western Dutchess along the Hudson River, emphasize this history of overt organizing and political action. We might call this the trail of public antislavery. In 1834, just one year after the formation of the national AASS, local abolitionists created the Poughkeepsie Anti-Slavery Society (PASS).[12] Articles 2 and 3 of the organization's constitution state clearly their purposes.

Constitution & Names of the Members of the Poughkeepsie Anti-Slavery Society

Article 2. The fundamental principles of this Society are that slavery is a stain upon our national character, that it is founded on injustice and is consequently a sin, that to be silent & inactive is a tacit assent to its perpetual existence and a national evil while a powerfull moral influence is the only weapon which might be used against it.

Article 3. The principal object of this Society is to exert & endeavor to increase this moral influence till it is coextensive with our common county and thereby effect the entire abolition of slavery.

(Note: One hundred twenty one citizens signed the constitution as members.)

Communities of faith took the lead in this work of "moral influence." They now included members of newly founded African Methodist Episcopal (A.M.E.) Churches in Fishkill and Poughkeepsie (see sites #7 and #9), as well as First Congregational Church in Poughkeepsie (see sites #8 and #11). Rev. Philetus Roberts, minister of the First Christian Church in Stanford, served as a president of the Dutchess Anti-Slavery Society. He supported a statement calling for citizens to support the Underground Railroad, as did "the Rev. Mr. Barber of Amenia," Rev. William N. Sayer of Pine Plains, and Rev. Frederick Tuckerman of Poughkeepsie. This suggests the key role of churches in fostering antislavery support (though the vast majority of local churches did not take such a stance).

Dutchess regularly sent interracial delegations to state and national abolitionist conventions. Notices in antislavery newspapers also show that such famous antislavery lecturers as Frederick Douglass and Abby Kelley Foster visited Dutchess repeatedly to speak and organize. An address of national significance, by abolitionist Angelina Grimké, appears to have taken place at Poughkeepsie's Colored Lancaster School (site #10).

On 31 July 1838, according to local reports, Poughkeepsie abolitionists helped to organize a local antislavery society in neighboring LaGrange. The most prominent abolitionist family there was the Sleight family. Solomon Sleight organized petition drives in the area and became a leader in the Dutchess County Anti-Slavery Society, a countywide body created in the same year. Local antislavery societies also formed in Pleasant Valley and Fishkill. Stephen E. Flagler, a resident of Pleasant Valley, hosted the second annual meeting of the Dutchess County Anti-Slavery Society at his home.[13]

The Dutchess County Anti-Slavery Society

The minutes of the Executive Committee of the Dutchess County Anti-Slavery Society (DCASS) are still in existence at the New York Public Library, and they offer a window into the organization's work. In the fall of 1838 the DCASS decided to send a questionnaire to persons running for state office in the coming election. The executive committee then met to analyze the answers so they could decide for whom to vote. The answers of four candidates (Seward, Marcy, Booker and Lisson) were deemed not satisfactory. However, the answers of three candidates (Beckwith, Barculo, and Conklin) were approved and the Society voted to support them in the upcoming election.

The first annual convention of the Society was held on Monday, 7 October 1839, at the house of Daniel P. Eighmie in Washington Hollow. The organizers declared that they were meeting "for the purpose of discussing their political duties in view of the approaching election in connexion with the all absorbing question of American slavery." The notice was signed by members of the DCASS executive committee: William Jenney, William McGeorge, John L. Dusinberry, Solomon Sleight, Samuel Thompson, Ira Armstrong, Samuel R. Ward, David L. Starr, Thomas Austin, John Low, and Darwin Canfield.

The discussions at this convention produced a letter addressed "TO THE ANTI-SLAVERY ELECTORS OF DUTCHESS COUNTY," outlining the duty of abolitionists in the upcoming state elections. The executive committee of the DCASS adopted a resolution from the state society:

Resolved, That we will neither vote for, nor support the election of

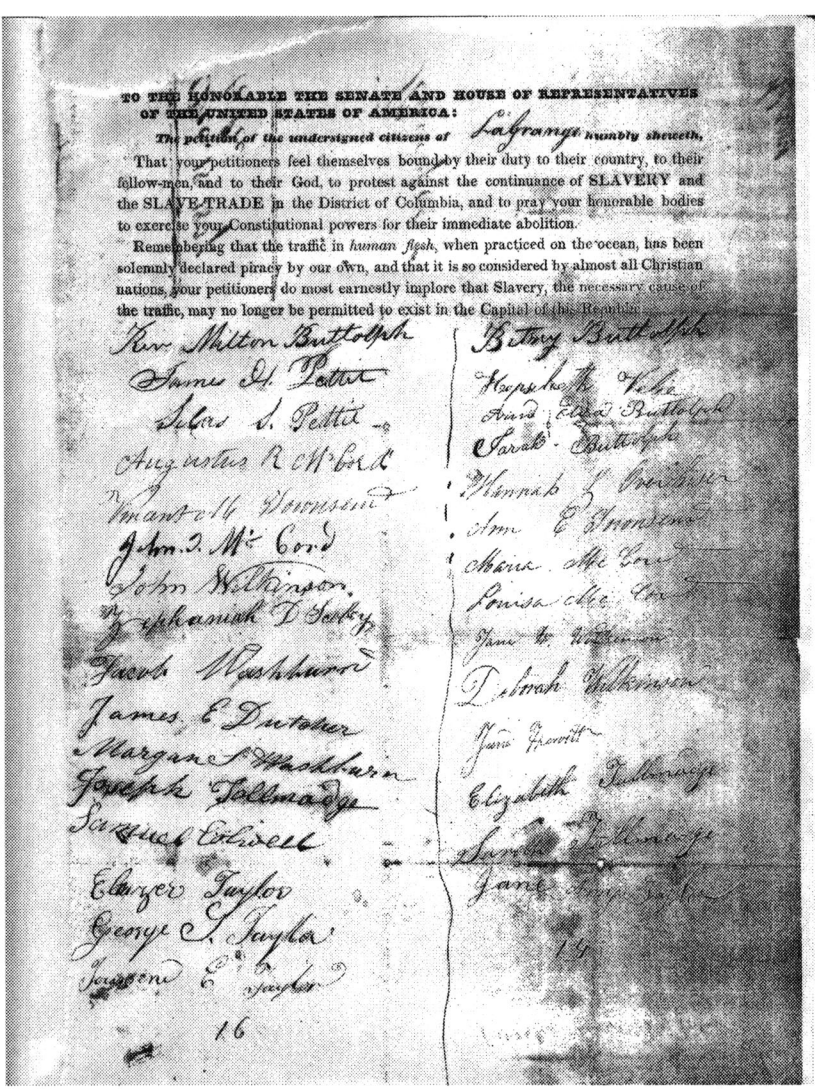

In 1838, citizens of LaGrange signed this petition to Congress, urging abolition of slavery and the slave trade in the District of Columbia. Men signed on the left and women on the right; women were active participants in petition drives, and petitions like these are an important tool for historians who are researching abolitionist women. Dutchess County abolitionists sent many petitions to the House and Senate, urging restrictions on the domestic slave trade, prohibition of slavery in federal territories, and outright abolition. In the 1840s, both Democratic and Whig leaders viewed such petitions as inflammatory and dangerous; they were automatically tabled without discussion. From the collections of the National Archives, Washington, DC.

any man for President or Vice President of the United States, or for Governor or Lieutenant Governor, or for any legislative officer, who is not in favor of the immediate abolition of slavery.... that IRA ARMSTRONG OF Poughkeepsie, SOLOMON SLEIGHT of LaGrange, and THOMAS HAMMOND, of Dover were thought worthy to receive the Anti-Slavery suffrage of Dutchess County.

Another broadside published by the Society also said it strongly: "WE SUPPORT NO MAN WHO VOTES AGAINST LIBERTY."

These were busy times for the DCASS. On 29 August 1839, the first issue of *The Bow of Promise* was published (the only issue extant). Its front page carried Article Three of the Constitution of the American Anti-Slavery Society: "This Society shall aim to elevate the character and condition of the people of color." Also included were the pledge of the New York State Temperance Society, an article entitled "The Bible Against Slavery," and a notice of the annual meeting of the New York State Anti-Slavery Society to be held in Utica at the Presbyterian Meeting House.

At the second annual meeting of the Dutchess County Anti-Slavery Society in June 1840, participants took a more radical stance. The broadside announcing this convention noted that it took place on Thursday, April 25, 1839, at the house of Stephen E. Flagler in Pleasant Valley. The broadside invited "All who feel an interest in the PRESERVATION OF THEIR LIBERTIES" to attend. An earlier brochure noted that Henry B. Stanton "and other distinguished gentlemen, and perhaps Gerritt Smith, Esq., are expected to address the convention." The rhetoric related to the meeting was strong:

> Freeman of the North! Farmers, Mechanics and Working Men! are you willing to see SLAVERY extended. The Slave-Holders say, that a Laboring People, bleached or unbleached, are a dangerous element of the body politic; that our Northern laborers, though nominally free, are in reality SLAVES; and that Slavery, in 25 years will prevail universally at the North! ! ! ! What do you think of such doctrines? ARE YOU PREPARED TO BECOME SLAVES? Come to the convention and hear further of this matter.

Participants in this convention adopted the following resolution:

> Resolved, that we collectively and severally will do all in our power to assist those of brethren, coming through this county, who may have thus far escaped the iron grasp of tyranny, by giving them meat, money, and clothes, to enable them to prosecute their journey to a LAND OF LIBERTY.[14]

This was the first public declaration by any group in the county of intent to engage in Underground Railroad activity. Newspaper coverage identified 23 participants in the convention. They included the pastor of Poughkeepsie's A.M.E. Church and several other pastors; two Poughkeepsie doctors; the Dutchess Academy's principal and a teacher at the school; six members of First Congregational Church; several Quakers; and several men who have not yet been identified, but who may have been African American residents (Marvin R. Armstrong, Henry Fairchild, and George LeRow of Poughkeepsie, and Charles Lacy of Hyde Park).

It appears that the Dutchess Anti-Slavery Society divided after 1840, as did the national movement, over the question of women's participation and the issue of whether to join the newly established Liberty Party. Local newspaper notices suggest, however, that despite the split, antislavery meetings and rallies continued locally throughout the 1840s.

This broadside advertised a Dutchess County antislavery convention, held at the home of Daniel Eghmie in Washington Hollow in 1839. Members of the Executive Committee of the Dutchess County Anti-Slavery Society are listed as signatories. From the collection of the Library of Congress.

Slavery and Antislavery 14

African American Activism in Poughkeepsie

While they cooperated with white allies in the antislavery movement, free Blacks in Dutchess County also organized their own societies for self-help and protest. They worked not only against slavery, but also for such diverse causes as public education, temperance, and African American suffrage in New York. The *Colored American*, an African American newspaper with subscribers throughout the North, reported one such meeting.

> "For the Colored American" – Poughkeepsie, June 21, 1840
> At a large and respectable meeting of colored persons held at Lancaster School…for the expression of sentiments in relation to the proposed Convention (of the New York State Anti-Slavery Society), and the claims of the paper called *The Colored American*. On motion Uriah Boston was chosen chairman, and James N. Gloucester was appointed Secretary; prayer being fervently offered by Rev. N. Blount of Connecticut. And whereas the long deprivation of this right (the elective franchise) has inflicted a wound in our soul…which is sinking deeper and deeper and cannot and will not be healed until the healing balm of a full and complete enfranchisement has been applied. Therefore it is with gratitude to God that we respond to the call for a state convention to be held in Albany, the 18th day of the coming August….

After 1834, African Americans also gathered each summer to celebrate British Emancipation Day. On August 1 in that year, Britain outlawed slavery in its West Indian colonies, including Jamaica, Barbados, and other sugar islands. This was a major milestone in the march toward abolition. Uriah Boston, a barber and African American community leader in Poughkeepsie, wrote to a New York newspaper reporting on one annual celebration.

Slavery in National Politics: Voices from Dutchess County

On 13 February, 1819, Dutchess County contributed an important voice in the debate over slavery's expansion into western territories. Congressman James Tallmadge, nearing the end of his single term as

Samuel Ringgold Ward was perhaps the most prominent African-American abolitionist who lived in Poughkeepsie. He taught at the Colored Lancaster School in the late 1830s and was ordained as a Congregational minister, out of First Congregational Church, of which he was a member. In the 1840s, Ward went on to become a nationally prominent lecturer and organizer against slavery.

a representative of the district, introduced in the House the famous "Tallmadge Amendment." In it, he proposed that Missouri Territory only be accepted as a state on stipulation "that the further introduction of slavery, or involuntary servitude, into the said State, be prohibited," and that all enslaved children born in Missouri after statehood be freed at age twenty five.

Tallmadge stressed that the Constitution did not permit Congress to end slavery in states where it already existed, and he acknowledged Southern fears that "servile insurrection" would result, if free states existed too near to those depending on enslaved labor. But Missouri was different, he argued: it was beyond the Mississippi River, and as "a territory acquired by our common fund," that "ought justly to be subject to our common legislation." The Tallmadge Amendment divided Congress on sectional lines, and the ensuing debate was bitter. The amendment passed the House but failed in the Senate; historians widely regard it as a critical turning point in the rise of slavery as a political issue.

Portrait of James Tallmadge by Freeman Hunt, published in Hunt's *Merchants' Magazine*, 1850

Tallmadge's impassioned speech was reprinted in the National Intelligencer. *February 15, 1819. The following is an excerpt.*

... Sir, the honorable gentleman from Missouri, (Mr. Scott,) who has just resumed his seat, has told us of the Ides of March, and has cautioned us to "beware of the fate of Caesar and of Rome." Another gentleman, (Mr. Cobb,) from Georgia, in addition to other expressions of great warmth, has said, that if we persist the Union will be dissolved; and, with a look fixed on me, has told us, "we have kindled a fire, which all the waters of the ocean cannot put out; which seas of blood can only extinguish!"

Language of this sort has no effect on me; my purpose is fixed; it is interwoven with my existence; its durability is limited with my life; it is a great and glorious cause, setting bounds to a slavery, the most cruel and debasing the world has ever witnessed; it is the freedom of man; it is the cause of unredeemed and unregenerated human beings.

If a dissolution of the Union must take place, let it be so! If civil war, which gentlemen so much threaten, must come, I can only say, let it come! ... The violence, to which gentlemen have resorted on this subject, will not move my purpose, nor drive me from my place. I have the fortune and the honor to stand here as the representative of freemen, who possess intelligence to know their rights, who have the spirit to maintain them. ... Sir, has it already come to this — that, in the Congress of the United States — that, in the legislative councils of Republican America, the subject of slavery has become a subject of so much feeling — of so much delicacy — of such danger, that it cannot safely be discussed? .. Are we to be told of the dissolution of the Union; of civil war, and of seas of blood? And yet, with such awful threatenings before us, do gentlemen, in the same breath, insist upon the encouragement of this evil; upon the extension of this monstrous scourge of the human race ? An evil so fraught with such dire calamities, to us, as individuals, and to our nation, and threatening, in its progress, to overwhelm the civil and religious institutions of the country, with the liberties of the nation, ought, at once, to be met, and to be controlled. If its power, its influence, and its impending dangers, have already arrived at such a point, that it is not safe to discuss it on this floor; and it cannot now pass under consideration as a proper subject for general legislation, what will be the result when it is spread through your widely extended domain? Its present threatening aspect, and the violence of its supporters, so far from inducing me to yield to its progress, prompt me to resist its march. Now is the time. It must now be met, and the extension of the evil must now be prevented, or the occasion is irrecoverably lost, and the evil can never be contracted.

Tallmadge's strong stance suggests that more research is needed on antislavery and its supporters in the Clinton area, where he inherited his father's substantial property, "Clinton Point." [15] *A notable Quaker father and son from Clinton Corners, Aaron and Townsend Powell, were both active abolitionists. In 1866, Aaron Powell became the editor of the* National Anti-Slavery Standard, *at a moment when abolitionists were debating what issues they should take up after Emancipation had been achieved.* [16]

Abolitionists in Dutchess sent petitions to Congress on a range of issues related to slavery and racial justice. Central among these was the fierce debate over whether to expand slavery into federal territories in the West, or to admit Texas, which was a major slaveholding area. Before the United States annexed Texas on 29 December 1845, as the 28th state, Dutchess County abolitionists protested the move. In a petition to Congress they requested "your honourable body not to admit any new state and to reject all applications and propositions for the annexation of Texas to the United States."

Local abolitionists also petitioned Congress for recognition of Haiti. In 1789, enslaved people on the Caribbean island of Saint Domingue had revolted against their French colonial masters, at a time when the island had over 500,000 slaves, mostly African born. During the Haitian Revolution more than 2,000 whites were killed and 180 sugar cane plantations destroyed. Finally, on 1 January 1804, Haiti was declared a free republic, but the United States – terrified that slave revolts would spread – refused to recognize or trade with the new nation. On 21 November 1838, a group of citizens from Pleasant Valley petitioned Congress that the undersigned, anxious that their country should cultivate a good understanding with all the established governments of the world, and especially with those which are founded on republican principles, "respectfully pray your honorable bodies to recognize in the usual form and manner, and to enter into the customary inter-national relations with the Republic of Haiti."

The Fugitive Slave Act of 1850: The Case of John Bolding

Antislavery sentiment intensified in the 1850s, particularly as Northerners organized to oppose the stringent federal Fugitive Slave Act of 1850. In the wake of this legislation, a number of famous cases arose, involving freedom-seekers across the North who were captured and returned to slavery. One of these cases involved tailor John Bolding of Poughkeepsie, who had apparently escaped from slavery with his younger brother David and a woman named Susan Moore. For more on this case, see the site of John Bolding's antebellum home in Poughkeepsie (site #12).

In 1860, the same year Abraham Lincoln won election to the White House, Dutchess residents voted into office some of the area's first outspoken abolitionists. Among them was James Bowne, Poughkeepsie's first Republican mayor. Local antislavery conventions continued even to the 1860s. One such convention was held in February 1860. Dutchess resident Lizzie DeGarmo, who was probably associated with the DeGarmo family of Crum Elbow Friends Meeting in Hyde Park, sent a report of this convention to the antislavery newspaper *The Liberator*.

Mar. 2, 1860
Mr. Garrison:
    Will you permit a stranger friend to occupy a small space in your columns for the purpose of informing your many listeners what a 'rich treat' we Poughkeepsians enjoyed, on the 23rd and 24th of last month. Our anti-slavery friends, Parker Pillsbury, Susan B. Anthony, Aaron M. Powell and Marius R. Robinson, held a convention in Concert Hall, Pokeepsie City, at that time; and the deep interest and attention manifested by the people present were heart cheering to those who have to wait and labor so long for "the good time coming." The speakers, as we all know, were of the highest order of talent and ability, and their discussions of the Slavery question, in all its varied aspects, were characterized by a clearness of insight, and an earnestness of purpose, that carried conviction to the hearts of their listeners.
    The resolutions offered by Parker Pillsbury, and defended by himself and Mr. Robinson, were of the most radical and revolutionary type, in both language and sentiment; yet no one ventured to question their

truthfulness and expediency, for the people are so thoroughly tired of this lukewarm opposition [to secession] so slavery in the Territories, while they are fostering and cherishing it at home, by carrying out the requirements of this slaveholding and slavery protecting government. It is a noticeable fact, and one worthy of remark, that the great Northern heart is every where beating with a more steady and healthful pulsation, since witnessing that noble and godlike sacrifice to principle, by John Brown and his associates, upon that Virginia scaffold, in November last; and although the lesson has been dearly learned, still it is not without its cheering results already; for it has shown us that with courage, heroic fortitude, and true Christian love, such firm reliance on God can give, when the trying hour shall come, when all gold must be tested in the Great Refiner's crucible.

The hall in which this Convention was held was a large one and the several sessions quite fully attended, considering how literally flooded the city has been with all kinds of lecture, thus far through the winter. There was a certain restiveness of spirit manifested by the pitiful apologists of the slave oligarchy, during the last evening, while the deeply probing artillery of Pillsbury's argument was pouring directly into the enemies ear at its most vulnerable point, showing them the utter recklessness to all the great interest of humanity, by their blind devotion to the Union and Constitution. Yet, notwithstanding this little outbreak, the meeting was a perfect success, and the friends of freedom have great cause for rejoicing at the gradual speed of the true Abolition doctrine. The occasion was truly one in which the soul pours itself out in silent thankfulness to God, that such true hearted men and women still live to bless humanity by their noble efforts in behalf of the downtrodden and oppressed.

There is yet one other cheering feature of this Convention, of which I wish to speak ere closing this communication, and that is, the numbers and intelligence of the colored people who attended its several sessions. Their number was proportionally large to that of the white people; and the interest and strict attention they manifested, joined to their quiet, orderly deportment, cannot help to reflect great credit to this much despised class of our citizens. Many of them are respected, and justly so, among us, as honest, upright business men and women and it does not seem possible that we should much longer tolerate that infamous decision, that declares that each of these 'have no rights that we, as God's children, are bound to respect.' Nor can we longer believe 'that institution to be beneficent, of God's ordaining, and for the best interest both the black and white race,' that so effectually blots out the manhood and womanhood of over 4,000,000 of our brothers and sisters, and converts them into chattels personal.

Truly yours for the right,
Lizzie DeGarmo

The work of Dutchess County abolitionists helped build a legacy of racial, social, and economic justice. By 1865, slavery crumbled as a result of the Civil War. The Thirteenth Amendment, ratified in the same year, ended slavery in all the states of the Union. It is appropriate that when the Dutchess Regiment (the 150th New York) returned home from Louisiana, many freedmen were reported to have accompanied them to Poughkeepsie. Others may have come north with the 128th Regiment, which served in Louisiana and Virginia before ending their tour of duty in Savannah, Georgia. African-Americans born in Georgia, Delaware, Maryland, Kentucky, Tennessee, Louisiana, Virginia, North Carolina, and Alabama were listed in the 1865 New York state census, suggesting that a striking number of Southern-born freedmen lived in Poughkeepsie by the war's end. [17]

Historic Sites Map 1

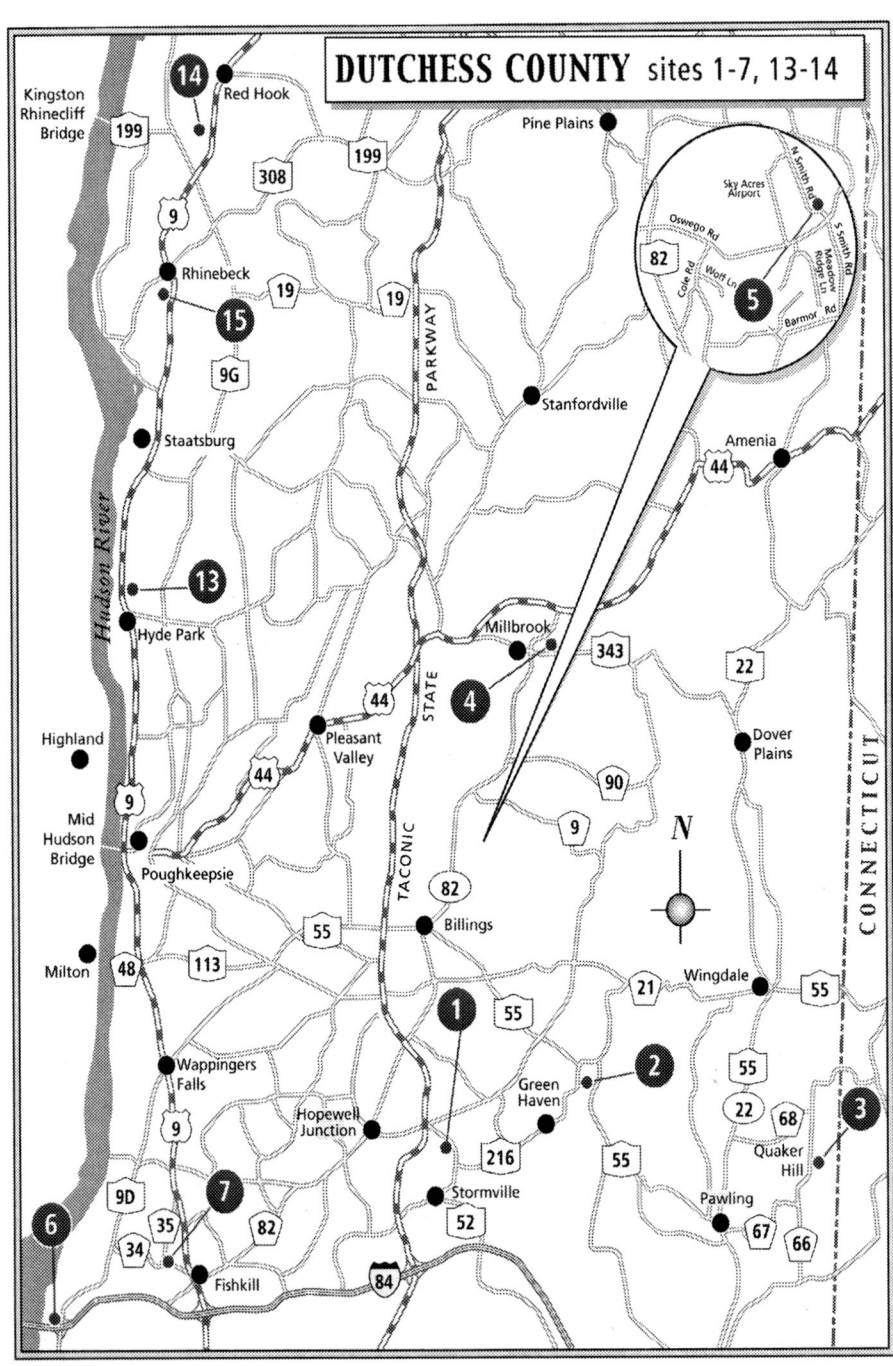

Slavery and Antislavery 22

Historic Sites Map 2

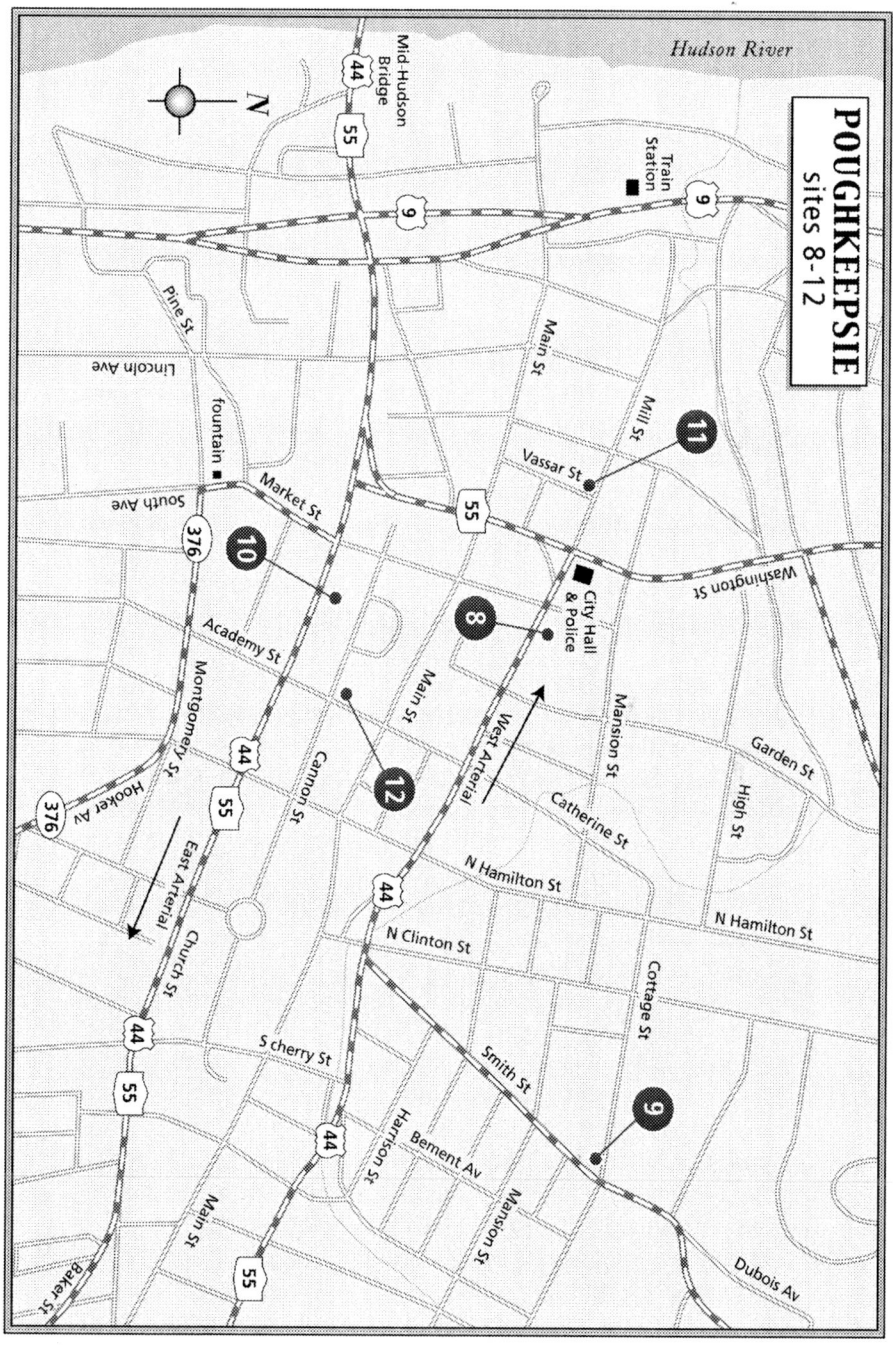

Slavery and Antislavery 23

Slavery, Antislavery and the Underground Railroad: Historic Sites in Dutchess County

The Quaker Trail to Freedom

1 **The Storm Family Slave Cemetery**
East Fishkill: NY 216; 0.6 miles north on Phillips Road

The Quaker Trail begins with the record of a slave community in Dutchess County: In 1739, Thomas Storm of Westchester County bought 400 acres of land in the Rombout Patent from Madam Catharyna Brett. The following year he moved his family there, and in the 1740s purchased another 400 acres in the area now known as Stormville. Upon his death in 1770, the land was divided among his children. Several branches of the Storm family used the cemetery to bury their slaves. The 1790 census lists 341 slaves, twelve of whom belonged to three Storm families. The 1820 census lists 838 African Americans in the Town of Fishkill, of whom 332 were slaves, eight registered under the Storm surname.[18]

A survey of old gravestones in Dutchess County in 1924 identified two headstones found in the cemetery, those of Betty Johnson (who died February 1, 1842) and Betty Moon (who died July 1, 1825). Betty Johnson's will was probated in 1848 and the inventory lists such items as a silk dress, three umbrellas, numerous quilts, a brass kettle, many books, a spittoon, her spectacles, a purse, and cash. One portion of the probated will lists several notes that were due from many of her neighbors, all of whom were white. She left an estate of $1,615.07 to her six siblings. Although the Storm Family Cemetery was thought to be a slave cemetery, the presence of Betty Johnson's headstone indicates that perhaps other free Blacks chose to be buried there at a time when African American burial grounds were typically separate from the cemeteries of their white neighbors.

In 2005 Dr. Brian McAdoo of Vassar College, at the invitation of the Dutchess County Historical Society, became involved in the preservation and restoration of the Storm Family Cemetery. After clearing the land, Professor McAdoo's students used sophisticated geophysical equipment to determine the boundaries of the cemetery and the possible number, depth and type of burial sites. Surveys found the burial ground to be approximately 51 meters long and 11 meters wide. Fifty-four marking stones indicated gravesites, although the number of graves could be 27 rather than 54, depending on whether both headstones and footstones were used. The researchers concluded that there were approximately 30 graves marked by stones.

This plaque, placed in 1985, marks the Storm Cemetery and its restoration.

Additional gravesites were identified through the use of ground-penetrating radar, which identified surface and sub-surface soil disturbances (anomalies) that might indicate the presence of graves. From the number of standing stones and anomalies, researchers estimated a total of between 30 and 80 graves.

In 1985, a coalition of concerned citizens made a first attempt to preserve the cemetery. Leaders of this effort included the Social Action Committee of the Smith Metropolitan A.M.E. Zion Church, the Mid-Hudson chapter of Omega Psi Phi fraternity, and the African American Heritage committee of the Catharine Street Community Center. A stone marker was placed at the site identifying the area as:

> Slave Cemetery
> The Storm Family
> 18th and 19th Century
> Donated by Presbrey Leland Monument Company

2 The Community of Freemanville
Poughquag: NY 216; Depot Hill Road

In the Town of Beekman, near the village of Poughquag, a free African American man named Charles Freeman established a community in the early 1800s. Very few freed black persons had sufficient resources to secure land. Charles Freeman was an exception, and the town of Freemanville became one of the most significant free African American communities in 19th century Dutchess County.

The 1800 census had 70 slaves and 56 free blacks living in Beekman. By the census of 1810 the ratio had changed dramatically, with 39 slaves and 104 free blacks living there. In 1800, Charles Freeman appeared as a free resident of the Town of Beekman, the head of a household of seven people. The 1810 census showed the Freeman family at the same site, with seven people and three cows. By this time, the family lived next to Samuel Dorland who was evidently also a free man as he had six free persons listed in his home and owned one cow. Two houses away from Dorland lived Anthony Ludlow, another free black man with three persons in the family. Several other families of free African Americans lived in Beekman in 1810: Jonas Coxsure with nine in the household, Robert Swan with three; Walter Lockwood with five; Edward Mason with five; and Lewis Baker with four. On June 2, 1831, Tanner, the daughter of Samuel Dorland, Nathan Miller and Daniel Brill witnessed Freeman's will. Although the Brill family had slaves, in 1817 Daniel

Brill's son John set free his slave Adam, at the age of twenty-nine.

By 1818 Freeman had purchased three acres of land for $312, and this became the nucleus for Freemanville.[19] The community began at the base of present-day Depot Hill. In its early days the area was pejoratively referred to as "Nigger Hill." Charles Freeman and his family owned land that stretched from Beekman into West Pawling. Between 1830 and 1840 the African American population of Beekman grew by almost 24%, and presumably most of these families clustered around the land of Charles Freeman. Michael Groth, in his study *Forging Freedom in the Mid-Hudson Valley: The End of Slavery and the Formation of a Free African American Community in Dutchess County, 1770-1850*, notes that while the population of the county declined in the second quarter of the nineteenth century, the free Black communities of Freemanville, Lithgow in the Town of Washington, Guinea Town in Hyde Park, and Baxtertown two miles west of the village of Fishkill grew during this period.

Among African American residents, Charles Freeman was unique in amassing the money needed to purchase land in Beekman in the early nineteenth century. He was also unique in the fact that he left a will: dictated on June 3, 1831, it was one of the few wills of free black persons filed in the Surrogate Court of Dutchess County. To his wife Sibble, Charles left his house for use until she died, and then it was to be divided among the children. To his eldest son, Sylvenus, he left land in Freemanville commonly called "the peach orchard." The filing with the Surrogate Court was so unusual that the witnesses had to provide affidavits that the signatures were actually their own. Thirteen persons were involved in probating the will, which was eventually proven on July 24, 1849. The family included:

    Sibble Freeman, wife of Charles
    Sylvenus Freeman, son
    Ebenezer Freeman, son
    Charles Freeman, son
    Egbert Freeman, son
    Helen Freeman, daughter and wife of Joseph Northrup
    Jane Freeman, daughter
    Cynthia Freeman, wife of Harvey Tawlman
    Sally Freeman, wife of Henry Wheeler
    Susan, only daughter of Martha Brister, deceased

daughter of testator (that is, Charles Freeman's granddaughter)
Emanuel Dorland, husband of Susan Brister

3 Oblong Friends Meeting House
Pawling: Just off DC 66 on Meeting House Road

Eastern Dutchess County had a substantial Quaker population in the 18th and 19th centuries. The community of Friends at Quaker Hill was the first stop for fugitive freedom-seekers traveling through Eastern Dutchess. The Oblong Meeting was authorized by the Friends Meeting at Purchase, New York, in 1744. In 1742 a committee was appointed to determine the dimensions of a meeting house to be built at the Oblong. The original meeting house was built across the road from the present one; in fall 1778 the Army of the Revolution camped here, and many soldiers are buried in the Oblong Cemetery.

On April 16th and 17th, 1764, two deeds of land were transferred to representatives of the Oblong Meeting "to be applied to the use and only service of the Society of the people called Quakers, to build and erect a meeting house or meeting houses." Membership growth was so rapid that a new meeting house was needed and a petition sent to the quarterly meeting at Purchase for a new building. The cost was 680 pounds, to be raised by other meetings of the Yearly Meeting.

As early as 1767, Quakers at Oblong Meeting raised questions about the relationship of Quakers to slavery. As one later historian analyzed the situation,

> Quakers saw in slavery harm to both the slave and the slaveholder. Slavery meant denying people the liberty to be obedient to the leaders of the Inward Light. As for the slaveholders, they found themselves constantly beset by temptations to laziness, violence, and exploitation, all of which were antithetical to the achievement of the holiness that brought salvation.[20]

In April 1767, the Oblong meeting forwarded a resolution to the Purchase Quarterly meeting: "Dutchess County Friends raised the issue

Slavery and Antislavery 28

of the 'Inconsistency of Slave Keeping with our Religious Principles.'"
The question was carried to the Quarterly Meeting in Purchase, and on
May 2, 1767, the group adopted the following:

> In this meeting the practice of tradition in Negroes, or other slaves,
> and its inconsistency with our religious principles was revived, and
> the inconsiderable difference between buying slaves or keeping
> them in slavery we are already possessed of, was briefly hinted at
> in a short Query from one of our Monthly Meetings.

The quarterly meeting delayed pressing the issue because it was thought
that such a resolution would divide the Society, but the meeting did insert
words to admonish the members. They sought to convince confirmed
slaveholders to give up their human property, arguing that "Negroes are
rational creatures." [21]

It took another nine years (until 1776) before a resolution decided that
meetings should not receive services nor accept financial contributions
from any Friend holding slaves, and eventually led to the disowning from
membership "those belated Friends who had not yet got their consciences
awake to the evil of owning persons." However, some Friends continued
to own slaves and it was not until 1779 that all Oblong members were said
to be without slaves. Five years after the Oblong meeting had achieved
their goal of being a meeting without any slaveholding members, all
American yearly meetings had ruled that members who owned slaves
must make arrangements to free them or lose membership.[22]

Between 1818 and 1828 the teachings of Elias Hicks created a split in
the Quaker movement. Each meeting was forced to choose the yearly
meeting with which they would affiliate. The Oblong Meeting became a
Hicksite Meeting in 1828.

One of the most prominent Oblong leaders was David Irish, a Quaker
preacher and an avid protestor against slavery. Irish was born on Quaker
Hill 20 June 1792, and died there on 2 October 1884. He and his family
joined the widespread boycott of slave-made sugar and cotton: the family
made maple syrup to take the place of cane sugar, and used nothing
but homespun linen and woolen clothing. David Irish subscribed to the
first antislavery paper published in the country, *The Genius of Universal*

Emancipation, edited by Benjamin Lundy, and he wrote antislavery articles for *The Friends Intelligencer*.

According to a turn-of-the-century testimony by Irish's daughter Phoebe, the family's home was always opened to welcome runaway slaves fleeing north. The Irish family fed and lodged such freedom-seekers, gave them words of encouragement, and gave directions to the next station on the Underground Railroad, most likely in Connecticut.

Oblong Friends Meeting

Tradition relates that David Irish occasionally kept a fugitive for a time and employed him or her, if he deemed it safe. According to his daughter, David Irish "never felt free to join with Anti-Slavery Societies outside of his own meeting, believing that by so doing he might compromise some of his testimonies, but with tongue and pen he labored zealously… to work against the sin of slavery." [23]

As the 19th century progressed, membership in the Oblong Meeting diminished. In the year following the death of David Irish, 1885, the meeting was "laid down." On May 28, 1936, the New York Annual Meeting of the Religious Society of Friends sent a letter to the Historical Society of Quaker Hill and Pawling, proposing that the title to the premises and the Oblong Meeting House along with the money and securities held for the benefit of the Meeting House be transferred to the Historical Society.

David Irish wrote several fiery letters to the Friends Intelligencer, *urging all Quakers to unite against slavery. The excerpt below is from a letter written on "22nd of ninth month," that is, September 22, 1858, and published in the* Intelligencer *that same month, pp. 487-8.*

He who can contemplate the wrongs of the slave and the iniquities of the masters with feelings of indifference, may justly suspect himself as wanting not only in regard for the good of his fellow men, but in one important characteristic of a disciple of Christ. "By this shall all men know that ye are my disciples, if ye have love to one another"— and this love leads its votaries, to "undo the heavy burdens, break every yoke and let the oppressed go free." If this subject claimed individual attention proportionate to its importance, the hearts of the people would pulsate in a right direction for its extinction.

To keep the system from observation and scrutiny is the slaveholder's hope and safeguard. Nevertheless, the effects produced by it are such as should induce in every one desirous of dealing justly and loving mercy, a candid inquiry, how far we have washed our hands in innocency in respect to the downtrodden slave. . . . While it is cheering to believe that the number of those who abstain from slave-labor products are on the increase, it is cause of surprise that the increase is not greater; because this mode of advocating the cause of the slave, is so far from interfering with other proper and consistent modes, that as an 'axe laid to the root of the corrupt tree,' it would impart weight and efficiency to them.

Every honest man disdains the idea of knowingly purchasing stolen goods of the robber, upon the principle that it would be approving and encouraging the act. But, alas! how few hesitate to purchase slave produce of the master merely because he has robbed the slave according to the forms of the law. How often do we hear the declaration, "I see no way that anything can be done at present for the abolishment of slavery." Is not this precisely the slave-holder's declaration? Are we about to adopt his conclusions, and follow his example? . . . If it was ever necessary not to be participants in the sins of Babylon, in order that we may escape her plagues, is it not now?

Interior, Oblong Friends Meeting, preserved largely as it would have appeared in the nineteenth century.

 Nine Partners Friends Meeting House
Millbrook: Junction of NY 343 and NE corner of Church Street

This area, known as Mechanic, was settled around 1750 by Quakers, who organized the Meeting in 1769 as a separate monthly meeting from Oblong (above). Following the lead of the Oblong Friends, the Nine Partners Meeting took a firm stand against the slave trade. In 1769 the meeting disowned Joseph Hustead for buying a slave even though he knew that the purchase was "contrary to Friends' principles." In 1774 the meeting appointed a committee to visit slaveholding members to "administer such advice as Truth shall direct" and report to the Meeting on the result.[24]

Just east of the Nine Partners Meeting House was the Nine Partners School (no longer extant), the first co-educational boarding school in America, and ancestor of today's Oakwood Friends School in Poughkeepsie. The school was possibly the most significant abolitionist institution in this part of the Hudson Valley. It had a profound influence on students who went on to shape the national antislavery movement and other great reform causes. They included abolitionist and women's rights advocate Lucretia Coffin (Mott) and her future husband James Mott, who chaired

The Nine Partners School, predecessor of today's Oakwood Friends School in Poughkeepsie, was a noted co-educational Quaker institution. The original school building, adjoining the Nine Partners Meeting, is no longer extant.

the Seneca Falls convention on women's rights. Another student was Daniel Anthony, later a stationmaster on the Underground Railroad, and father of Susan B. Anthony. The school's headmaster Jacob Willetts, and his wife Deborah, were Quakers and member of the Nine Partners Meeting. It appears that the Willetts often received freedom seekers, probably from the Oblong Meeting. Their home still stands, not far from the Meeting House, and is marked with a historical sign.

James Mott and Lucretia Coffin Mott were among the early teachers at Nine Partners. Both later became nationally prominent abolitionists and Lucretia became a well-known advocate of women's rights.

Excerpts from questions offered by the teachers in the Nine Partners Boarding School, to their Pupils, and the answers given by them. The Scholars had the liberty of referring to books for aid, when they found themselves unable to give proper answers without such assistance. Published in Danville, VT, by Daniel Lowell, 1815.

Are there any slaves in the United States? Some of the New England states have proved that they consider all mankind "free and equal" by not allowing slavery in them; the middle states have provided for their gradual emancipation; but in the southern part of the Union, this dreadful evil and all its baneful effects, prevail to an alarming degree.

Do Friends hold slaves? There were formerly instances of it, but at present there are none.

Do they countenance or promote slavery in any way? If using such articles as are produced by the labor of slaves, is countenancing, or promoting slavery, we are not clear of it; but there are some amongst us who believe it is right to abstain from those things.

On May 16th, 1848, the committee charged with the care and oversight of Nine Partners Boarding School reports that the Nine Partners Meeting is undertaking to boycott slave-made products:

> The subject of the use of slave labor in the Institution claimed the attention of the committee, and Friends were united that the superintendents be requested to procure, as far as practicable, all articles of Free Labor for the use of the Institution, agreeably to the course of the yearly meeting.

Some researchers have noted that a Free Black community was located in Lithgow, not far from Nine Partners, in the eastern area of the Town of Washington. Possibly that community played some role in moving fugitives around the Quaker Trail in eastern Dutchess to freedom in the north. There is no precise location for the settlement in Lithgow; research is continuing.

5. Oswego Friends Meeting House
Moore's Mill: NY 82, 1.2 miles east on Oswego Road at intersection with S. Smith Street

The land on which the Oswego Meeting House stands was purchased in 1751 and deeded to Jesse Irish, National Yoemans, and Allan Moore. The Meeting was an offshoot of the Oblong Meeting in Pawling in 1758, and the Meeting House building dates from 1760. After the liberal Hicksite Friends and the more Orthodox Friends split in 1828, Orthodox Friends in the Oswego area met in homes and finally in 1861 moved to Poughkeepsie and began their own meeting. (There was also a Hicksite Meeting in Poughkeepsie.)

The area near the Oswego Meeting House was known as Moore's Mill and was the home of Stephen Haight and Alfred and Charlotte Haight Moore. According to oral history, all engaged in Underground Railroad activities. The daughter of a Friend at Nine Partners reported that freedom-seekers were sometimes taken from Nine Partners and Moore's Mill to Valentine Hallock's house, located just south of Poughkeepsie, on the road that led to the Milton horse ferry.[25] This house would now be on Sand Dock road (Route 48) just south of the IBM complex. Hallock, a

---

In addition to the Oblong, Nine Parners and Oswego Friends Meetings, other religious institutions also expressed their concerns about the fact that slavery was incompatible with their beliefs. Amid the turmoil of the American Revolution, members of the North East Baptist Church undertook a debate that produced this remarkable document. (The church still exists today at 1 South Maple Avenue in Millerton.)

September the 24, 1778, the Church being met together and after prayer to Almighty God for his Gracious presence and assistance the Church proceeded to consider the matter Concerning the Slave Trade as Brother Reynolds and others had manifested their burden about it and after some considerable conversation about the manner of their being slaves and holding them as such the Church looks upon it to be depriving their fellow men of the liberty that Almighty God had given to all men Contrary to the gospel and vote that they would not have anything to do to uphold it.

Milton Ferry, from Benson J. Lossing, *The Hudson*, 1866. This ferry was one of the last "horse ferries" on the Hudson; it was operated by two horses stepping on a set of pedals that in turn powered a wheel, carrying the boat across the river. Quakers in Dutchess are said to have used this ferry to help those escaping slavery to reach Milton, where there was a large community of Friends.

Quaker, grew up in Marlborough, Ulster County, and his family were prominent leaders of the Friends' Meeting in Milton. Thus, fugitives may have been routed across the Hudson River on the Milton ferry, where they could be sheltered by Quakers of the Milton Meeting.

The River Trail to Freedom

 Mount Gulian Historic Site
Beacon: NY 9D; Lamplight St. becomes Sterling St: 145 Sterling

Mount Gulian was the home of the Verplanck family of Dutchess County. Mount Gulian is not known to have been an Underground Railroad site but is an important site on the River Trail due to its close association with James F. Brown, an escaped slave who left an unusually

Slavery and Antislavery 36

After securing his freedom, Richard Jenkins, described as a "Bard Negro" (presumably enslaved as property of the Bard Family) became the sexton at St. James Episcopal Church in Hyde Park. He appears, right, in this mural in the Hyde Park Post Office, completed in the 1930s under auspices of the Works Progress Administration.

The Nine Partners School, operated by Friends in Millbrook and a prominent local site of antislavery activity. When this image was acquired by the Oakwood Friends School, it was accompanied by a paper stating that this was "a drawing of the School at Nine Partners made circa 1812-1814 by student Eliza Jordan who was born in 1800 and became a recorded minister in the New England Yearly Meeting." From the archives of Oakwood Friends School, courtesy historian Kathy Moyer.

Smith Metropolitan A.M.E. Zion Church is the oldest African-American church in Poughkeepsie. It was originally formed in 1836 as the African Methodist Episcopal Church on Catharine Street, and from its founding served as a locus of education, community organizing, and civil rights advocacy. Many of the church's early members were active abolitionists.

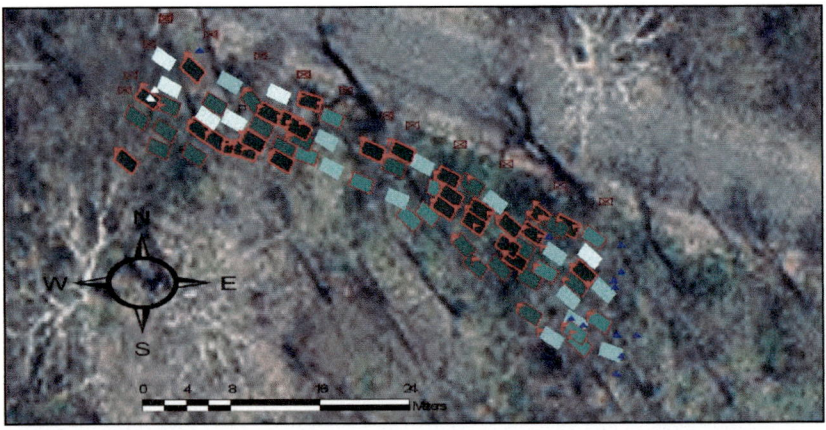

Likely gravesites at the Storm Cemetery, as determined in a 2005 survey by Dr. Brian McAdoo of Vassar College, and student researchers

Notice of an antislavery convention in Pleasant Valley in April, 1839. Dutchess County Antislavery Society, Manuscripts and Archives Division, The New York Public Library, Astor, Lenox and Tilden Foundations.

Lithograph of First Congregational Church, Poughkeepsie, as it appeared around the time it was dedicated in 1859. Many early members of the church were active abolitionists. Often in cooperation with Quakers and with members of the A.M.E. Church on Catharine Street, they organized petition drives and attended national and state antislavery conventions.

rich historical record.

James F. Brown was born into slavery in Fredericktown, Maryland, in 1783. Escaping to New York he was hired by the Verplanck family who purchased his freedom. From 1827 to 1866 Brown was the family gardener. Later Brown purchased the freedom of his wife Julia who was still in Maryland. Beginning in 1829 "Brown kept a personal diary (10 volumes) in which he meticulously recorded gardening chores, plant experiments, weather conditions, his personal affairs and those of his wife, and the changing times along the Hudson River between Fishkill Landing and Newburgh." [26]

Mt. Gulian Historic Site, the Verplanck home and home to freedom-seeker James F. Brown. The site is open and tours of the house, barn, and garden are available (for a fee) on Wednesdays, Thursdays, Fridays, and Sundays from 1 to 5 pm, from mid-April to the end of October. For more information visit www.mtgulian.org.

One scholar examining the diaries notes that David Ruggles, the leader of the New York Vigilance Committee made at least one visit to see James Brown at Mount Gulian.[27] Ruggles had several connections with Dutchess County. In 1833 he was listed as a "delegate from Poughkeepsie" in the records of a national convention. Samuel Ringgold Ward, a minister of the First Congregational Church of Poughkeepsie, had earlier been Ruggles' secretary. Ward had come to Poughkeepsie to replace Nathan Blount, the principal of the Colored Lancastrian School in Poughkeepsie.

7 The Community of Baxtertown
Fishkill: DC 35; Opposite 272 Osborne Hill Road

Baxtertown was originally a settlement of free blacks and Wappingers Indians, believed to have been at one point the largest community of free Blacks in Dutchess County. The Baxtertown Methodist Episcopal Church was the center of community life. Among the inhabitants a lively church life centered around grove meetings, picnics and plenty of work. Although it has not been proven, Baxtertown was purportedly a station on the Underground Railroad.

Tradition tells that there was an Indian reservation nearby and gradually the two groups merged. A 1937 study noted:

> Some of the first Negro settlers were slaves in Fishkill families, others had bought their freedom or had come north on the Underground Railroad. The land on which they settled was rocky or marshy, unfavorable to agriculture. The community cemetery is located on Osborn Hill Road, with markers dating to 1832. One marker is in memory of James Gomer, who had been a slave in the family of Professor Charles Davis for 42 years.

In the early 1840s James Gomer held Sunday afternoon Bible classes in his home in Beacon. On August 26, 1844, these students formally organized the Colored Methodist Episcopal Ebenezer Church. In his diary James Brown (gardener at the Verplancks' Mount Gulian) in an entry on Tuesday, May 28, 1844 noted "John Peter Dewint has presented to the coloured people of Fishkill Landing a lot to build a Methodist Church." In another diary entry of Sunday, September 1844, he documents the dedication: "The

St. James A.M.E. Zion Church as it appears today

Slavery and Antislavery 38

Coloured Methodist Church at Fishkill Landing dedicated by the Rev. Mr. Rush of New York City. The day warm." James Gomer was the founder of this new church of Fishkill Landing. This church was later named the St. James African Methodist Episcopal Zion Church of Beacon, New York, in honor of its founder.

Since African American churches were an important part of life in Dutchess County, James Brown, in his diary, mentions several times attending "Zion Church Fishkill Landing."

Gravesites of James and Sally Gomer, who were among the founding members of the St. James Church. James Gomer was a local freedman.

8 First Congregational Church of Poughkeepsie
City of Poughkeepsie: 269 Mill Street/US 44 West

First Congregational Church, 269 Mill Street, and its congregation played a leading role in the local abolitionist movement. The church formed after a February 1837 incident, in which the Poughkeepsie Anti-Slavery Society invited Samuel Gould, a lecturer for the American Anti-Slavery Society, to speak in Poughkeepsie at the Second Presbyterian Church. A mob attended the lecture, shouted and roared to stop Gould's speech, and then surrounded the pulpit and threatened him with violence. Gould took refuge at the home of Dr. Thomas Hammond, the Poughkeepsie abolitionist who was hosting him. Reportedly, the mob broke all the windows in Hammond's home before dispersing.

When leaders of several local churches failed to take a strong stand against the attack, some of their members "came out" to create First Congregational. They purchased the former sanctuary of Second Presbyterian, at the corner of Mill and Vassar Streets (see site #11). In 1850 FCC sold this property and constructed a new sanctuary at 269 Mill Street.

Of the first 73 men who joined First Congregational, at least 40 were documented members of local antislavery societies. The church rulebook required all members to oppose "the buying or selling of human beings or holding them in involuntary servitude." Of twenty-three persons who signed the resolution against slavery at the second annual meeting of the Dutchess County Anti-Slavery Society in June 1840, six were members of the First Congregational Church: Thomas Austin, Ira Armstrong, John Low, Samuel Thompson, James Van Wagner, and William M. West.

Many members of this church were local shopkeepers and merchants. Armstrong and Austin both operated shoe stores on Main Street. James Bowne was a dry goods merchant; Samuel Thompson was a sashmaker; James Hervey Dudley was a master carpenter who became a self-taught architect, while William M. West was a chair manufacturer. Captain Jeromus Wiltsie was a passenger barge captain on the Hudson. Theodorus Gregory, who had come to Poughkeepsie in 1831 from Rensselaer County, operated Poughkeepsie's temperance hotel, The Gregory House, located at 343 Main Street, at the corner of Catharine

Street. Along with Gregory, a number of other fellow abolitionists – both black and white – were active in the cause of temperance, which was another great reform movement of that day. Less is known about women in the congregation, but many in the Thompson, Cable, and other families appear to have signed women's antislavery petitions.

In 1839 First Congregational extended membership to Samuel Ringgold Ward, a freedom-seeker and abolitionist of national significance. Born in slavery on the eastern shore of Maryland about 1817, he escaped as a small child with his parents and settled in Greenwich, New York. Ward came to Poughkeepsie early in 1839 to teach at the Colored Lancaster School (see site #10). In May 1839 he was ordained to preach by the Congregational Association when it met in Poughkeepsie. Also in that year he became a traveling agent for state and national antislavery societies; soon after, he took up a pastorate in upstate Wayne County. The *New York Times* once described Ward as "the ablest and most eloquent black man alive," and abolitionist Frederick Douglass later wrote that "as an orator and thinker Ward was vastly superior, I thought, to any of us." Deeply embittered by the failure of the United States to move toward abolition and racial justice, Ward and his family left the United States in 1855 for Jamaica. He died in poverty there a few years later. [28]

On the eve of Abraham Lincoln's inauguration in March 1861, FCC pastor Rev. Moses Coit Tyler preached a remarkable antislavery sermon, which provides further evidence of FCC's strong antislavery stance. Tyler called for "no further concessions to slavery." "If adhering to the right will not save the Union then the Union is not worth saving." He boldly argued that "while disunion and war and devastation are a great evil, there is yet one evil, evermore and everywhere infinitely greater" – that is, slavery. [29]

James Dudley and Charlotte Wiltsie Dudley were prominent members of First Congregational Church. Both the Dudleys were active abolitionists and James, like many FCC members, was a founding member of the Poughkeepsie Anti-Slavery Society.

9 Smith Metropolitan AME Zion Church
City of Poughkeepsie: 124 Smith Street off US 44 West

The A.M.E. congregation was first founded in 1836 as the United Society, after African American members withdrew from the Washington Street Methodist Episcopal church. The Society met in the schoolhouse of the Lancaster Society and named its church the African Methodist Episcopal Church of Poughkeepsie. From its founding, the church and its leaders played prominent roles in the local antislavery movement.

In 1840 the church moved to 102 Catharine Street (near today's Beulah Baptist Church) and was incorporated as the First African Methodist Church of Poughkeepsie, New York. The church served as a focal point for celebrations of such events as West Indies Emancipation Day and other antislavery activities. One account of Emancipation Day in the 1840s reported that "a few minutes before 11 o'clock a procession was formed at the A.M.E. Church, on the top of Catharine Street, and marched to the steamboat landing to receive and escort the delegations to the festival that were expected from the towns up and down the river." This was followed by a parade to College Hill where Frederick Douglass addressed the crowd.

According to *The Colored American*, 8 June 1839, Rev. J. N. Mars was at that time pastor of the AME Church. He and Uriah Boston are listed in *The Colored American*, 30 January 1841 as the two Poughkeepsie sales agents for the newspaper. Boston was one of the original trustees of AME Church and a regular contributor to *The Colored American* newspaper in New York City. He arrived in Poughkeepsie in 1837 from Lancaster, Pennsylvania. After an apprenticeship with Jared Gray, another active member of the AME Church who had a barbershop at 290 Main Street in the 1840s, Boston established his own barbershop. Listings for his barbershop in city directories locate it at 12 Garden Street in the late 1840s, and later at 286, 292, and 254 Main Street.

Boston was one of the most frequent correspondents from Poughkeepsie to *The Colored American* and also published letters in Frederick Douglass' Paper. His obituary in the *Dutchess Courier*, 16 June 1889, noted "that year after year the various questions of the day, and especially that of anti-slavery, were discussed at Boston's tonsorial rooms." Boston's wife,

Nolis, was active in Emancipation Day activities and other meetings in the Black community.

Several other prominent abolitionists were associated with the AME Church. Rev. Nathan Blount was a cofounder of the church and the first teacher at the first school for African American children, the Colored Lancastrian (or Lancaster) School. He was a founding member of the Poughkeepsie Anti-Slavery Society and later served on the executive committee of the Dutchess County Anti-Slavery Society. Blount served as a delegate to national antislavery conferences in New York City in 1837. At a meeting of the DCASS on 6 November 1839, Blount tendered his resignation due to his appointment "by the Providence of God" as minister over a congregation in Providence, Rhode Island.

Smith Metropolitan AME Zion Church

Isaac Deyo and his family were also prominent in the AME Church. Deyo, a founding member of the Poughkeepsie Anti-Slavery Society, was listed in the 1845 *Poughkeepsie City Directory* as living on Jefferson Street, and in 1850 on Mansion Long Row. John A. Cole, a founding trustee of the AME Church, was a member of both the Poughkeepsie and Dutchess Anti-Slavery Societies.

On July 16-17, 1863, during the Civil War, the AME Church on Catharine Street served as a meeting placed for a statewide convention of African Americans who drafted a resolution calling on New York to give Blacks the right to bear arms in order to abolish slavery. During the same summer, when draft riots erupted in vicious mob attacks on Blacks in New York City, similar violence emerged in Poughkeepsie. Members of the Catharine Street Church armed themselves and patrolled the area around their property, but mob violence resulted in the governor calling in the Vermont Volunteers to restore order.

In 1910 the current church was constructed at 124 Smith Street, supported by a $20,000 donation from William W. Smith of the Smith Brothers Cough Drop Company. "Zion" was added to its name at that time.

10 The Lancaster School
City of Poughkeepsie: 189 Church Street/US 44 East

The building at 189 Church Street (now the Ciboney Café) once housed Poughkeepsie's first known school for Black children, the African Free School, a private school formed in 1829. Isaac Woodland was the first teacher at the school from 1829-1830.

The site of the Lancaster School as it looks today.

During the mid-1830s the Lancaster Society, which operated a school for poor white students in the Church Street building and had exclusive domain over "public education" in the village, took control of the African Free School and allocated a room on the second floor. Nathan Blount remained the teacher. In April 1839 the trustees certified Blount as a "respectable citizen and a well-qualified, competent, and thorough teacher of youth." [30] Blount served from 1830 to 1839.

When Blount resigned to become the pastor of a church in Providence, Rhode Island, the trustees hired Samuel Ringgold Ward to take his place. Ward (see site #8) taught in the Lancaster Colored School for a brief period.

Slavery and Antislavery 44

A year after Poughkeepsie created a united public school system in 1843, the Lancaster Society ceased to operate its white and black schools. The Poughkeepsie School Board created a separate Colored School No. in 1844. On May 6, 1844, a primary black school was opened in the Primitive Methodist Church on Mansion Square. After a short period this school was moved to the AME Church.

A critical event in American antislavery history and women's history apparently occurred in the Lancaster School building. In antebellum America, it was not thought proper for women to speak before "promiscuous" public audiences – those made up of both women and men – though it was acceptable to teach other women in parlor settings. American Anti-Slavery Society lecturer Angelina Grimké believed, however, that women had a duty to speak publicly against slavery. She and her sister Sarah, daughters of a wealthy South Carolina slaveholder, had converted to Quakerism and moved North. In Poughkeepsie, in March 1837, Angelina Grimké became the first white woman in the United States to speak on a political topic to an audience of both men and women. After this meeting she begin to speak regularly to mixed-gender audiences, precipitating heated debate in the abolitionist movement over the role of women. Grimké's work was a crucial factor in the emergence of women's rights activism within antislavery ranks.

Angelina Grimké c. 1844

Angelina Grimké to Sarah Grimké, 3 April 1837

We spent yesterday week in Poughkeepsie & brother [Gerritt] Smith & ourselves had a meeting with the colored people in the evening. About 300 attended, & it was a very satisfactory meeting I believe to all parties & for the first time in my life I spoke in a promiscuous assembly, but I found that the men were no more to me then, than the women. Some of the females present were very desirous we should hold a meeting with the ladies, & we would gladly have done so, had we not expected to leave town early the next morning. [31]

Lancaster School 45

11 Second Baptist Church
City of Poughkeepsie: Corner Mill and Vassar Sts. off US 44 W

From 1838 to 1859 this building was the site of the First Congregational Church. It was at this location that American Anti-Slavery Society lecturer Samuel Gould was mobbed; Frederick Douglass spoke here in 1847, at the invitation of the Congregational Church, when he was denied a platform at City Hall. (No local newspaper deigned to cover Douglass' address.) It is probably at this location, also, that Rev. Samuel Ringgold Ward was ordained as a Congregational minister.

Second Baptist Church in Poughkeepsie, formerly the site of First Congregational

12 Former Site of Home of John Bolding
City of Poughkeepsie: 20 Academy Street off US 44 East

John Bolding was apparently born into slavery on a plantation near Columbia, South Carolina, owned by a slaveholder named Townsend Dickinson. Dickinson hired Bolding out, but when Dickinson's health declined, Bolding was sold to the service of two other men, Ernest and Robert Anderson. Bolding somehow escaped from slavery around 1840, apparently accompanied by his younger brother David and an enslaved woman named Susan, who married an African-American Poughkeepsie tailor named Francis Moore.[31]

The Moores, John Bolding and David Bolding are listed in the 1850 census, living in the same household; Susan Moore and John and David are all listed as having been born in South Carolina. Their residence was located at 20 Academy Street. The house on that site was apparently razed a few years later to build the Lady Washington Fire House, now home to the Children's Media Project. The Moore/Bolding tailor shop was located at 4 Liberty Street, beside the Main Street hotel run by local abolitionist Theodorus Gregory (near Uriah Boston's barbershop).

Gravesite of John Bolding at Poughkeepsie Rural Cemetery

In 1851, after passage of a harsh new federal Fugitive Slave Act, a white visitor from South Carolina recognized Bolding in Poughkeepsie and alerted his former master. In August 1851, Bolding was seized at his shop by US Marshals, whisked to New York City, tried in a special federal court (rights of habeus corpus had been suspended in such cases, on the presumption that those captured were in fact slaves, and slaves did not have such rights). Bolding was sent back to slavery to South Carolina. The case became a national sensation - one of the more than a dozen infamous instances of enforcement of the Fugitive Slave Act.

Citizens of Poughkeepsie, led by local abolitionists, raised funds to pay for Bolding's freedom. His owner agreed to accept $1,750 in payment but then demanded an additional $250 for transportation expenses. Though it was first considered doubtful that this sum could be raised, local abolitionists succeeded in doing so by November. Bolding returned to Poughkeepsie and lived there with his wife, Henrietta, until his death. In the post-Civil War years they lived at 14 Pine Street.

13 St. James Episcopal Church, Hyde Park
Hyde Park: 4526 Albany Post Road (US 9)

St. James Episcopal Church of Hyde Park was founded in 1811 by Dr. Samuel Bard with the Reverend John McVikar serving as the first pastor, 1811-1817. Church confirmation records indicate that Blacks were early congregants of St. James. In 1814 three blacks were confirmed (Jack Lenin, Sally Lenin, and Nancy Bard). In 1817 three blacks were confirmed (Sarah Maize, Amy Ray and Janie Lenicks). In 1819 Donald Clarke and Sukey Peters were confirmed, and in 1830 five additional blacks were confirmed (Eliza Cable, May Cox, Richard Jenkins, Jane Riddles, and Susan Maclean).

Nearby was "Guineatown Lane," home of many Black families. St. James records indicates that in 1828, ten students registered in the church's Sunday School lived in Guineatown. The class roll book also states that Nathan Blount, the teacher at the Lancaster Colored School in Poughkeepsie (see site #10) was the Sunday School teacher. An 1837 floor plan of St. James documents that church pews were rented to families. However, two pews located in the back of the church were marked

St. James Episcopal Church in Hyde Park

"Free," near the pew marked "Free Sexton." Richard Jenkins was the first sexton and held this position for 45 years until his death in 1857; he had been enslaved and was property of the Bard family. For his faithfulness he was given a family burial plot in the churchyard. Thus, among the graves of prominent Hudson River families are the graves of Richard,

Slavery and Antislavery 48

his wife Nancy, his daughter Susan Mary Johnson Jenkins, William Jenkins, and Griffin Jenkins. Also there is the grave of Harry Anthony (died 1866, age 82) who became the sexton after Richard Jenkins. Most of the written information about this community is provided from the writings of a Hyde Park resident, Edward Braman, in 1876.

In the fall of 2007 Dr. Brian McAdoo, Vassar College Department of Earth Science and Geography, and his students from Vassar College surveyed a part of the St. James Cemetery with ground-penetrating radar, a magnetometer, to locate possible black grave sites in the southeast corner of the cemetery. A community legend had indicated that blacks were also buried in unmarked graves in the cemetery. The study concluded that no geophysical anomalies were located there, supporting the conclusion that no unmarked graves were located in that area.

Gravesite of sexton Richard Jenkins, a freedman, who was the church's first sexton

An archaeological study of the Guinea community is being conducted by Dr. Christopher Lindner, Archaeologist in Residence at Bard College. The Guinea Archaeology Project is sponsored by the Dutchess County Historical Society and the Town of Hyde Park, with the support of Bard College, the Dyson Foundation, and other funding sources. The study estimates that the Guinea community existed from approximately 1790 to 1870. Approximately 60 individuals have been identified who lived there. Among them were Primus Martin and Artemis Quackenbush. Quackenbush, a freed slave probably from the Pawling area, was a member of Saint James Episcopal church. The Primus Martin house was a small dwelling measuring 9 feet by 16 feet. The Guinea site is closed to the public to protect this valuable historical resource.

14 The Quitman House, Rhinebeck
Rhinebeck: 7015 US 9; 0.6 miles north of intersection of 9/9G

In this study we primarily examine the words and actions of abolitionists. It is important, however, to look at the best known of the slaveholders in order to set these in context: the majority of white residents of the Hudson Valley supported slavery.

John A. Quitman was born and raised in this house, as the son of Rev. Frederick H. Quitman and Anna Elizabeth Hueck Quitman. He trained for the ministry but then moved to Ohio, where he passed the bar. Moving to Natchez, Mississippi in 1821, he established a successful law practice there and married into a wealthy

John A. Quitman, from a portrait done while he was serving as Governor of Mississippi

The Quitman House as it appears today. In cooperation with the Rhinebeck Historical Society, the house is open from 2 to 4 pm on Saturdays and Sundays from mid-June through October. For more information visit www.quitmanpreservation.org.

Slavery and Antislavery 50

family. He eventually came to own four large landholdings near Natchez: three cotton plantations and one sugar plantation. At peak, around 1850, Quitman owned between 400 and 500 slaves.

In the 1840s, Quitman led Mississippi troops in the Mexican-American War; returning a war hero, he ultimately became governor of Mississippi in 1850. In that post he urged Mississippi voters to secede, and in 1852 he ran for U.S. vice president on the Southern Rights ticket. He was prosecuted in federal courts, soon afterward, for his role in a military attack on Cuba, which he hoped to add to the Union as a slave state. This prompted his resignation as governor. Quitman died at his Natchez mansion in 1852.[32]

There is scanty evidence to show Quitman's relationships with slaves while he lived in Dutchess County. It is known, however, that his father, Dr. Frederick Quitman, "owned several slaves."[33] When Quitman first went south he made several observations in a letter: "These...are the happiest people I have ever seen.... These Southern slaves are indeed to be envied." Once he entered Mississippi politics, Quitman became a fiery secessionist and a fierce apologist for the "peculiar institution."

15 Rhinebeck Cemetery
West side of Mill Street (US 9); 0.3 miles south of intersection with NY 308

Entering the Cemetery from the gates on Mill Street, proceed up the section known as the Summit and continue down hill; there is a section with few stones that is the Black or Colored Cemetery.

The Rhinebeck Association Cemetery opened in 1845 after town authorities prohibited burials in the village's churchyard. On August 27th, 1853, Miss Mary Garrettson gave a half acre of ground in the cemetery for the burial of "people of color." Miss Garrettson, born in 1794, was the daughter of Catherine Livingston (sister of Chancellor Livingston) who in 1793 married Rev. Freeborn Garrettson, a well-known Methodist minister who freed his slaves in 1775, when he was called to be a minister. An only child, Mary never married; she lived at Wildercliff, the family home in Rhinebeck, after the death of her father in 1827 and her mother in 1849.

Miss Garrettson died in 1879 but this gift of land was incorporated with many others over the years to be organized into one cemetery. The Black cemetery area, located in Section E, was identified as "Potter's Field." Among the tombstones in Section E, one bears the inscription, "Jack – Native of Africa – Death October 17, 1826." Nearby are the burial sites of the Frazier family, a black family well known in the town of Northeast. The stone in memory of Andrew Frazier (1743-1846) notes his service in the Revolutionary War. Frazier lived in Milan; he died at age 102.

We invite you to consider, in this place, the threads that connect Dutchess County to the wider history of America and the world. At this site, a native of Africa is buried. Not far away are old colonial estates along the Hudson, where enslaved men and women long labored; even nearer by is the childhood home of John Quitman, one of the South's wealthiest slaveholders and an architect of secession. The courageous men and women, here in Dutchess, who organized against slavery did not confront a theoretical threat. Slavery was woven into the fabric of Hudson Valley life from the very start. It is thus even more remarkable that African Americans and whites, women and men, Quakers and other people of faith, overcame their differences and joined together in an interracial movement, leaving a legacy for us today in their vision of freedom and equal rights.

African American burials at the Rhinebeck Cemetery

Slavery and Antislavery

Notes

[1] For this and other information on enslaved and free African-Americans in Dutchess see Michael Groth, *Forging Freedom in the Hudson Valley: The End of Slavery and the Formation of a Free African-American Community in Dutchess County, New York, 1770-1850*, Ph.D. dissertation, SUNY Binghamton, 1994. See also "Sources and Suggested Reading" at the end of this guide.

[2] Groth, *Forging Freedom in the Mid-Hudson Valley*, esp. 145, 179.

[3] This document is in the New York State Library, Albany.

[4] Groth, *Forging Freedom*, chapters 4 and 5.

[5] Hugh Barbour, Christopher Densmore, Elizabeth H. Moger, Nancy C. Sorel, Alson D. Van Wagner, and Arthur J. Worrall, eds., *Quaker Crosscurrents* (New York: Syracuse University Press, 1995), 65.

[6] Ibid., 21.

[7] Ibid., 59.

[8] Fergus M. Bordewich, *Bound for Canaan: The Underground Railroad and the War for the Soul of America* (New York: Amistad, 2005); on women, especially, see Julie Roy Jeffrey, *The Great Silent Army of Abolitionism: Ordinary Women in the Antislavery Movement* (Chapel Hill, NC: University of North Carolina Press, 1998).

[9] Moses Roper, *Narrative of the Adventures and Escape of Moses Roper* (Berwick-upon-Tweed, England, 1848), p. 45-6; *Poughkeepsie Eagle*, 27 December 1860.

[10] *Poughkeepsie Eagle*, 20 July 1874.

[11] *Greenville News*, 13 July 1996.

[12] Before that date, David B. Lent served as the first known Dutchess correspondent for state antislavery organizations. Lent, apparently a Quaker, was a harness-maker who lived at 83 Smith Street in Poughkeepsie and owned considerable property east of town.

[13] *The Friend of Man*, 31 July 1838. Solomon Sleight's obituary appeared in the *Poughkeepsie Journal* on 8 March 1843.

[14] *Poughkeepsie Journal*, 3 June 1840.

[15] See Yoshawnda L. Trotter, "James Tallmadge," *American National Biography*. Ed. John A. Garraty and Mark C. Carnes (New York: Oxford University Press, 1999).

[16] James Talmadge, Congressional Speech, February 15, 1819 (Washington, D.C.: *National Intelligencer*) February 1819.

[17] Duane A. Biever, *Old Poughkeepsie* (N.p., D. A. Biever, 1997).

[18] Sara Mascia Ph.D., David Martin, Daniel Zivin. *Documentary and Field Study, Storm Cemetery, East Fishkill, Dutchess County, New York*, Appendix 3. Prepared for WCI Communities, by Historical Perspectives, Inc., Westport, CT, October 2007. The full report is on file with the New York State Office of Parks, Recreation, and Historic Preservation, Bureau of Historic Preservation, Peebles Island, Waterford, New York.

[19] Dutchess County Deed Records, Liber 2, p. 580.

[20] Thomas D. Hamm, *The Quakers in America* (New York: Columbia University Press, 2003), 34.

[21] Arthur J. Worrall, *Quakers in the Colonial Northeast* (Hanover, NH: University of New England Press, 1980), 163.

[22] Hamm, *The Quakers in America*, 35.

[23] Phoebe Wanzer, David Hicks, 10.

[24] Michel Groth, *Forging Freedom in the Mid-Hudson Valley*, p. 72.

[25] Dutchess County Deed Records, 1853, Liber 98, p. 331.

[26] A. J. Williams-Myers, *Long Hammering: Essays on the Forging of an African American Presence in the Hudson River Valley to the Early Twentieth Century* (Trenton, New Jersey: African World Press, Inc.), p. 175

[27] Dr. A. J. Williams-Myers, State University at New Paltz.

[28] Sernett, Milton C. "Ward, Samuel Ringgold." *American National Biography*. Ed. John A. Garraty and Mark C. Carnes (New York: Oxford University Press, 1999).

[29] Moses Coit Tyler, "Our Solace and Our Duty in this Crisis," Samuel J. May Anti-Slavery Collection, Division of Rare and Manuscript Collections, Cornell University Library, http://dlxs.library.cornell.edu/m/mayantislavery/index.htm

[30] *Colored American*, 1 June 1839.

[31] Kathryn Kish Klar, *Women's Rights Emerges Within the Antislavery Movement* (Boston: Beford/St. Martin's Press, 2000), 96-97.

[32] "John Bolding, Fugitive Slave." *Dutchess County Historical Society Yearbook* (hereafter DCHSY) 20 (1935): 51-55; "Arrest of Another Fugitive Slave," *New York Herald Tribune*, 26 August 1851; "Bolding a Free Man," *Liberator*, 21 Nov. 1851; for obituaries of Bolding and his wife, see various Dutchess newspapers on 1 and 2 May 1876, and *Dutchess Courier*, 12 March 1884.

[33] For a detailed study of Quitman's role as a slave master, see Robert E. May, "John A. Quitman and His Slaves: Reconciling Slave Resistance with the Proslavery Defense," *Journal of Southern History* 46 (1980): 553-570. See also Robert E. May, "John Anthony Quitman," in *American National Biography*, ed. John A. Garraty and Mark C. Carnes (New York: Oxford University Press, 1999).

[34] J.F.H. Claiborne, *Life and Correspondence of John A. Quitman: Major General, U.S.A, and Governor of the State of Mississippi* (New York, New York: Harper and Brothers, 1860), 28.

Sources and Suggested Reading

Primary Sources used in researching this guide included the following newspapers and documents; also recommended are the research libraries of the Dutchess County Genealogical Society/LDS Library (particularly membership records of Friends Monthly Meetings), the Dutchess County Historical Society at Clinton House, and the Local History Room at Adriance Library, all in Poughkeepsie.

The Colored American
Dutchess Courier
Frederick Douglass' Paper
The Friend of Man
The Liberator
National Intelligencer
Poughkeepsie Eagle
Poughkeepsie Journal
Poughkeepsie Telegraph
Poughkeepsie City Directories, 1843-1860
United States Census, Poughkeepsie, Dutchess County, New York, 1830-1870.

"The Antislavery Movement in Dutchess County." *Dutchess County Historical Society Yearbook 1943*, pp. 57-66.

"John Bolding, Fugitive Slave." *Dutchess County Historical Society Yearbook* (hereafter DCHSY) 20 (1935): 51-55.

Biever, Duane A. *Old Poughkeepsie, 1865*. N.p., D. A. Biever, 1997.

Bordewich, Fergus M. Bound for Canaan: *The Underground Railroad and the War for the Soul of America.* New York: Amistad, 2005.

Claiborne, J. F. H. *Life and Correspondence of John A. Quitman: Major General, U.S.A, and Governor of the State of Mississippi.* New York, New York: Harper and Brothers, 1860.

Colarco, Tom. *The Underground Railroad in the Adirondack Region.* New York: McFarland, 2004.

Crane, Susan J. "Antebellum Dutchess County's Struggle Against Slavery," *DCHSY 1980* (65): 35-43.

Dutchess County New York Anti-Slavery Society, Manuscript Collection 868, New York Public Library.

Griffen, Clyde and Sally. *Natives and Newcomers: The Ordering of Opportunity in Mid-Nineteenth Century Poughkeepsie.* (Cambridge, MA: Harvard UP, 1978).

Groth, Michael E. "Forging Freedom in the Mid-Hudson Valley: The End of Slavery and the Formation of a Free African-American Community in Dutchess County, New York, 1770-1850." Ph.D. dissertation, SUNY Binghamton, 1994.

----------. "The Struggle to Build a Free African-American Community in Dutchess County, 1790-1820." *Hudson Valley Review* 14.2 (1997): 14-34 + corrections.

Hamm, Thomas D. *The Quakers in America* (New York: Columbia University Press, 2003), 34.

Hasbrouck, Frank. *The History of Dutchess County, New York.* Poughkeepsie: S.A. Matthieu, 1909.

Jeffrey, Julie Roy. *The Great Silent Army of Abolitionism: Ordinary Women in the Antislavery Movement.* Chapel Hill, NC: University of North Carolina Press, 1998.

Mabee, Carleton. "Separate Black Education in Dutchess County." *DCHSY* 65 (1980): 5-20.

Mascia, Sara Ph.D., David Martin, Daniel Zivin. Documentary and Field Study, Storm Cemetery, East Fishkill, Dutchess County, New York, Appendix 3. Prepared for WCI Communities, by Historical Perspecives, Inc., Westport, Ct., October 2007.

Mamiya, Lawrence H., and Lorraine M. Roberts. "Invisible People, Untold Stories: A Historical Overview of the Black Community in Poughkeepsie." *DCHSY* 72 (1987): 76-104.

McCracken, Henry Noble. *Blithe Dutchess: The Flowering of an American Community from 1812.* New York: Hastings House, 1958.

Platt, Edmund. *The Eagle's History of Poughkeepsie, 1683-1905* (Poughkeepsie: Platt and Platt, 1905).

Roper, Moses. *Narrative of the Adventures and Escape of Moses Roper*. Berwick-upon-Tweed, England, 1848.

Sernett, Milton C. "Ward, Samuel Ringgold." *American National Biography*. Ed. John A. Garraty and Mark C. Carnes (New York: Oxford University Press, 1999).

Shaughnessy, Edward J. "The Last Train to Coffin Hill." Mss. in possession of MHAHP.

Sklar, Kathryn Kish. *Women's Rights Emerges Within the Antislatery Movement*. Boston: Bedford/St. Martin's Press, 2000.

Smith, Philip H. *General History of Dutchess County from 1609 to 1876*. Pawling: Philip H. Smith, 1877.

Still, William. *Underground Rail Road*. Philadelphia, 1872; reprinted New York: Arno Press, 1968.

Trotter, Yoshawnda L. "James Tallmadge." *American National Biography*. Ed. John A. Garraty and Mark C. Carnes. New York: Oxford University Press, 1999.

Tyler, Moses Coit. "Our Solace and Our Duty in this Crisis." Samuel J. May Anti-Slavery Collection, Division of Rare and Manuscript Collections, Cornell University Library. http://dlxs.library.cornell.edu/m/mayantislavery/index.htm

The Underground Railroad in Central New York: A Research Guide. Online at http://www.oswego.,edu/ugrr/guide.html

Upton, Dell T. "Dutchess County Quakers and Slavery, 1750-1830," *DCHSY* 55-60.

VerNooy, Amy P. "Antislavery in Dutchess County." *DCHSY 28* (1943): 57-66.

Wanzer, Phoebe T.. "David Irish: A Memoir." Read at the third annual meeting of the Quaker Hill Conference, 7 Sept. 1901). Reprinted 1967, Historical Society of Quaker Hill.

Ward, Samuel Ringgold. *Autobiography of a Fugitive Negro*. (Available online at Documenting the American South website, UNC Chapel Hill.)

Wellman, Judith. "The Underground Railroad and the National Register of Historic Places: Historical Importance vs. Architectural Integrity." *Public Historian* 24 (Winter 2002): 11-29.

Williams-Myers, A. J. *Long Hammering: Essays on the Forging of an African-American Presence in the Hudson River Valley to the Early Twentieth Century.* Trenton: Africa World Press, 1994.

----------. *On the Morning Tide: African Americans, History and Methodology in the Historical Ebb and Flow of Hudson River Society.* Trenton: Africa World Press, 1993.

----------. "The Underground Railroad in the Hudson River Valley: A Succinct Historical Composite." Afro-Americans in New York Life and History, 2003. The Free Library (online).

Worrall, Arthur J. *Quakers in the Colonial Northeast.* Hanover, NH: University of New England Press, 1980.

Young Armstead, Myra B., ed. *Mighty Change, Tall Within: Black Identity in the Hudson Valley.* Albany: SUNY Press, 2003.